CW00847590

DEE DELSY

A Lover Just Like Me

Copyright © 2022 by Dee Delsy

All rights reserved. No part of this publication may be reproduced, stored or transmitted in any form or by any means, electronic, mechanical, photocopying, recording, scanning, or otherwise without written permission from the publisher. It is illegal to copy this book, post it to a website, or distribute it by any other means without permission.

Dee Delsy asserts the moral right to be identified as the author of this work.

Email: lovers@writeme.com

Scripture quotations marked (MSG) are taken from THE MESSAGE, copyright (C) 1993, 2002, 2018 by Eugene H. Peterson. Used by permission of NavPress, represented by Tyndale House Publishers, a division of Tyndale House Ministries. All rights reserved.

Scripture quotations marked (TLB) are taken from The Living Bible copyright (C) 1971. Used by permission of Tyndale House Publishers, Carol Stream, Illinois 60188. All rights reserved.

Scripture quotations marked (NIV) are taken from the Holy Bible, New International Version (R), NIV (R). Copyright (C) 1973, 1978, 1984, 2011 by Biblica, Inc. TM Used by permission of Zondervan. All rights reserved worldwide. www.zondervan.com

Scripture quotations taken from the Amplified (R) Bible (AMP). Copyright (C) 2015 by The Lockman Foundation. Used by permission. www.lockman.org.

Scripture quotations marked (DAR) are taken from the DARBY BIBLE, published in 1867, 1872, 1884, 1890; public domain

Scripture quotations marked (GW) are taken from GOD'S WORD(R) Copyright (C) 1995 by God's Word to the Nations. All rights reserved.

First edition

This book was professionally typeset on Reedsy.
Find out more at reedsy.com

Contents

Dedication

Written to YOU,
With LOVE.

All Around Us

All around us, all around us
    You've created relationships
    All around us
That signifies your relationship
All around us
From the ecosystem in the natural environment
All around us
To the creations and inventions of man
All around us
You're trying to help us comprehend You
All around us
You're desperately reaching out to us
All around us
If only we could stop and see the connections
All around us
Then it would be so easy to understand your love
From inside of us.

Introduction

M any things makes God different from us, undoubtedly so. This book does not explore that as there are enough literature to enlighten us on these. Instead, we examine how proximal we are to God and He to us. Through generations, God is expressed to man in many thematic forms, many that rightly reflect how distinctly different He is from us. In this book, we examine God's principal quality, love. What is love? It is the foundation of our creation, the principle guiding our existence, and the basis for things we see and know around us.

Humans are relational beings. We are social, seek fellowship, and enjoy one another's company in different ways and forms. How does God socialize and relate to us? How is He similar to us? What does God hear and say? Does He feel? How does He react and express His emotions?

God is love. This concept is not new. It always has been, it always will be. His love is not seasonal, conditional, or erratic; it is constant. His care is not provisional; it's complete. His love for humans is untamable. It rages continually on His inside. He made us to love us, to be expressions of Himself in both sexes.

God's love is an exciting dimension of who He is. It bears uncanny resemblances with how we experience and give love as humans. Just like us, our God is a hopeless romantic. Psalm 8 v4 (TPT) describes how the writer could not understand why God would bother with mortal men or be infatuated with us. Note the word "infatuation" here. It's for a reason. Infatuation is the early stage of love where everything is perfect, and the other can do no wrong. God is hopelessly in love with us, and it's almost like He can't stop Himself.

I hope that as you read this book, you discover how God is a lover, just like you, and that, in reality, we are closer to God than we might think.

What is Love?

As a verb, love is an action. Love is most powerful when it's active. To love is to do. There are different expressions of love in relationships and families: from sleepless nights for the parents of a newborn to giving up personal hobby time for shared activities. Love is also displayed in taking children to after-school activities after a full day's work to missing out on fun time with friends so you can nurse an ailing relative. Expressions of love exist all around us—in different ways and varying degrees.

Our Heavenly Father has expressions of love we can relate to as well. The most significant one was offering up His only son, Jesus, to be born as a man and die the worst kind of death for us all. This profound sacrifice is God's love in action.

To provide some background for people who have no idea about Christianity, in the beginning, when God created man in His image, he had free will to be able to demonstrate His love for God. As part of this free will, he was required not to eat a particular fruit as a code of conduct. This code is similar to the ones we have in societies that govern our morality and behavior. Codes of conduct like not breaching peace with public fighting; not shoplifting from a store; to more grave ones such as not robbing or not terminating a life. To make a long story short, the first man, Adam, ate this fruit and set the justice system running. This act of dishonour or contempt introduced a dimension of hardship and vulnerability to humans. It gave God's opponent (guess who this is?) the right of way into humanity, perverting the perfectly planned course of life originally intended by God for us all.

God came up with a wonderful retrieval plan to resolve this and re-instate humans to their original heritage. This plan, however, would come at a price. The plan was to send Jesus to die for humans to reclaim us all and cause us to get back in alignment on His perfect course for our existence, which is to be loved by Him. God, the creator of the universe, infinite in His majesty, infinite in His glory and wisdom, devised a genius plan. He is the maker of the landscapes, from the hills to the mountains, from sea life to land life, author of seasons and time and carries unlimited power. Yet, he gave up His son to take up a mortal human body to be spat at, humiliated, unloved, unwanted, disregarded, and unsought.

I'm certain you've probably watched a movie or read a book or seen a TV series where someone wealthy came to penury, especially for something that wasn't their fault. Even worse than that is what I'm referring to. So, say, for example, Bill Gates, founder of Microsoft, had his consciousness transferred into one of his creations (an application)—say a Word document, and all other Word documents used around the world thought he was like them. But obviously, that's not the case; he's far more enlightened than all of them combined. He knows their purpose, programming, capabilities, strengths, weaknesses, activities that will make them stand out and shine. He is privy to the ones they were not designed to perform (like using MS Word for presentations, instead of PowerPoint or MS Word for analysis, instead of MS Excel. Straight away, we'll know that there will be profound limitations using MS Word in these circumstances). In this hypothetical example, let's assume that Bill, as the master-builder, had to have his consciousness transferred to get all Word documents all over the globe saved from a fatal virus out to corrupt or destroy them. Now imagine how constricting and unnatural it must be for him, someone who is used to making an app and other related systems, to now be confined into one of those creations to preserve them. Okay, I know that this example may not necessarily be the best, but hopefully, you get the essence.

Jesus came to the world, from walking on the streets of gold and having everything we see and do not see at His service to being born in penury. He grew up and died the worst kind of death people at His time could die—slow and excruciating corporal punishment by crucifixion.

This is the most remarkable and most significant expression of God's love, the basis for our unlimited communion and access to Him with others to be examined further in the book.

His Love

Created, made, fashioned, designed, bespoke, tailored. God's love is the reason we have come to be. Unlike some manufactured products that are designed to perform the same function with the unique identifiers being serial numbers to distinguish them, our lover, aka God, tailored us uniquely, with unique gifts, abilities, and circumstances, down to unique fingerprints, such that no two humans are ever the same. This is not an accident; it can't be.

His love picks us up from where we are, in whatever state we are, and like the many fairy tales with happy endings, transforms us into the best versions of ourselves. This love is fulfilling, beyond human description, because it is flawless. The closest analogies that we experience as humans are the feelings of true love between a couple and the overwhelming love for a newborn and children as they grow up. Because God instituted the family, He's patterned it after the kind of relationship He wants to have with us in its purest form. The flawless love of God for us helps us experience an over-the-moon feeling that causes all substitutions (sex, wealth, alcohol, career, etc.) to pale in comparison. That love and its accompanying feeling gives us the confidence to face our circumstances and prevail. That love empowers us to embrace our distinctiveness rather than trying to fit in. We're powerfully confident to be unique and be true to ourselves because we know He made us, He loves us, and we are always the first on His agenda for our lives.

Another truth about the love of God is that it's "everlasting." God loves us with an everlasting love, addressing the security need for love that we have as humans. It means that once we've accepted His love into our lives and have invited Him to be the captain of our lives, we can be confident that as He starts to lead and guide us in the way that we should go, He will make even the bleakest of circumstances turn around for our good. I turn to a fairy-tale analogy here because I think there are some profound truths of God's love in these stories, and they're so popular and easy to relate to.

Cinderella's story is applicable here. Cinderella, a mere mortal, was forced into slavery in her father's house (the earth). Her stepmother and stepsisters (the enemy, devil, sickness, affliction, pain, etc.) thought her value was permanently undermined. They had determined her future, and it certainly wasn't looking good.

I'm sure that there were times Cinderella would have believed their versions of her future. And, at these times, it must have looked bleak. But then the prince's (Jesus Christ) invitation came, with the help of the fairy godmother (the Holy Spirit), she entered the palace as a princess. She was experiencing her wildest dreams by moving away from slavery, obscurity, and lack of fulfilment to serving the needs of her kingdom, being in the limelight, and being fulfilled in love and purpose.

God's love is real. It's tangible; it's genuine, it lasts, it's complete, it's everything. It's the very reason we are made. It's why there's a void in the heart of humans that we try to fill with all sorts of things like wealth, fame, career, family, sex, control, etc. It's why there are so many religions, and it's why the belief that there is no God attempts to fill that void with self (proclaimed rationalized logical thinking).

I call it the **love principle**. It's why everything natural and man-made responds to love—humans, animals, and plants. This love principle is why tended houses continue to be habitable and deserted houses become dilapidated. The nurturing language of love is understood by everything and everyone—living and non-living—because it stems from the creator. To amplify this a bit more, it's like how inventors and manufacturers leave their seal on their products to distinguish them from others. Love is God's seal/signature. If it's not love, it's not God. Loves' principle resonates in our central human core. We were made to experience His love continuously, designed to be complete in Him, crafted to be the best of ourselves in His plan for us.

Love Serves

◦◦◦◦◦

The most extraordinary acts of inventions are acts of service. A conviction that there must be a better way of doing things has driven humans from cave dwellers to become masterminds of some of the most astounding, cutting-edge comforts of modern life we enjoy. In addition, humans have given themselves to causes all around the world driven by love.

True love serves. Starting from a relationship between a couple to that of a family to that of friends to that of employers to that of customers to that of people in positions of authority. Love serves by solving problems, and the complexity of the problem solved determines the reward. In the workplace, service is rewarded by a promotion (or higher delegation of duties) in most cases. A director is solving more complex problems for the organization or serving at a higher capacity than someone else in another role. Families and friends solve the problem of companionship and social interaction, employees and employers solve the customer's problems, cinemas solve the problem of entertainment, houses solve the problem of shelter, food solves the problem of hunger, etc. There is a transition to working in jobs or roles that we love, as it's proven that we perform better in these roles than the ones we're not endeared to.

Love's service is not without reward or payment. There are remunerations for our jobs, and we pay for the services we have used. So where there is service, there is a reward and the more excellent the service, the more excellent the reward and vice versa.

Just like us, our Heavenly Father serves us. I know! The first time I thought about this, it was mind-blowing. We live in cultures and societies that exalt being served over serving; this is a misunderstanding. Everyone serves, in one way or another, only in different capacities. Organizations serve their clients, and that's why they remain in business, politicians serve their nations, and that's why public opinion is important, employees serve their employers, parents serve their children, etc.

Every service is an act of giving, and in that giving is life and the receiving of a reward. Whoever does not give does not get; that's how life is designed. Serving is living. When we give our bodies food, we receive nourishment. When we give our bodies exercise, we receive fitness.

Remember that the greater the complexity of the problem solved, the greater the reward? Good. God solved the most complex problem of mankind, which is being lost without Him due to the fall of Adam. He solved this problem by the wonder of the cross, as outlined earlier. Love serves, and we are all givers and receivers with inexhaustible examples among us all. So, God serves (gives as demonstrated on the cross, to gain all of us to Himself) because this is how He receives, just like us.

Matthew 20: 26-28(MSG): "...Whoever wants to be great must become a servant. Whoever wants to be first among you must be your slave. That is what the Son of Man has done: He came to serve, not be served—and then to give away his life in exchange for the many who are held, hostage."

John 3:16(ICB):"For God loved the world so much that he gave his only Son. God gave his Son so that whoever believes in him may not be lost, but have eternal life."

Love Chooses

I t was the football game in school, and there were a few kids there. Each captain was selecting their team members, one team member at a time. *Oh, I hope I won't be the last one to be picked*, I thought to myself. One by one, the most promising team members were selected until I was the only one left. Begrudgingly, I was selected to be part of a team. I really couldn't blame the captain. I was not the best player. I looked and played weakly, but football was my passion, and I couldn't understand why I didn't have the talent for it.

I honestly thought I was a good dancer. I was part of a dance club in school, and on Fridays, we would dance as part of the practice sessions. During the dance lessons, I always gave it my hardest, which probably was part of the problem. Dance moves shouldn't be forced but should flow naturally and be graceful. However, I never got to perform at any event or competition. I didn't make it. I was not good enough to be chosen.

I don't know if we have stories like this that we can relate to, stories of things we're not so good at, boys we were attracted to at high school that never looked our way, or girls we dreamed about every night who were way out of our league. The point is, it sucks to be forced upon someone or not be considered worthy enough to be chosen.

God created humans as we are, rational, logical, emotional—all the things science and philosophy talks about—for a reason. He didn't want robots that were programmed to do his bidding, who had no choice whether to be with him or not. While initially, it may be exciting to have someone who does everything you want them to do, it gets boring with time because you're not sure what their real intention, choice, or motive is. That's where we come in. God made us with our own free will so that we can make a rational choice to choose Him. That's a big deal because He doesn't want to impose or force. He wants it to be mutual, both ways.

There was a time when it was the norm for parents to match their children in arranged marriages to their partners, not too far off in human history. However, at present, we mostly live in societies where each one finds their partner, one they have a connection to build a life with because having mutual affection in a loving relationship is essential.

Just like us, God delights in being chosen, and that's why throughout the Bible, His word demonstrates this. From the time He spoke to Abraham and gave Him a choice to follow Him, to His appearance to Moses to seduce him to be His chosen representative, to singling Paul out for the supernatural. Time and time, He gives the opportunity to choose Him and these are not only happenings recorded in the Bible, but are also real today. From the countless number of people who heard a sermon to those who are reading books like this one and discovering Him, to those who cry out to Him in their darkest hour asking Him to show up if He's real, to people who were born and raised in Christian homes. He continually wants us to choose Him and keep Him as the center of our lives. Not self, not wealth, not career, not lack, not anything. To trust Him with our being, to experience the best form of living there is—one where we shift our focus from ourselves so that we might find our true selves within Him. He wants to be chosen first, selected, preferred, just like us.

Revelation 3: 20 (MSG): "Look at me. I stand at the door. I knock. If you hear me call and open the door, I'll come right in and sit down to supper with you."

Love Trusts

O n a scale from 1 to 10, how would you rate the importance of trust in a relationship? Trust is the single most pivotal attribute that determines the balance in how lovers, people, and nations interact with one another. From nuclear weapons to create a sense of security for nations to broken families, divorce, and all the heartaches that come with it. From being given the freedom to work without imposing supervision to explosive or toxic vs calm and fulfilling relationships. Trust is the most crucial element.

We need trust. We need to know that the other person has us covered (got our back). At the same time, experience teaches us that gullible trust can be an undoing when the shock of the reality of a cheating spouse or the gruesome revealing of a "friend's" atrocities are revealed. Sadly, gullible trust, in some cases, has led to many untimely demises, examples we may be able to recall.

Healthy relationships thrive on trust. Signs of trust and the security it breeds can range from being able to use one's phone without being peeped on, the ability to go out without sniggering comments, the ability to express love sincerely without any manipulative undertones and conditions, amongst others.

Just like us, our Heavenly Father wants to trust us and wants us to trust Him. The Bible describes humans straying from the true God as cheating, and it stems from us not trusting Him. The biblical word for this is "faith." Without this, we can't walk with God without suspicions. There is, however, a fundamental difference between trusting God and trusting men or other alternatives (wealth, riches, honor, career, children, spouse, positions of authority, etc.). God is the creator of the heavens and the earth. He is the beginning and the end. He is the almighty God. He intricately knitted us to the minutest detail, our weaknesses, our greatest insecurities, our biggest confidences. He's fully aware, and He says, "I made you, I love you, you're perfect in my eyes," and He says, "Trust me, walk with me and watch me use these things that rock your confidence to bring you into [the] limelight." God says, "Have faith in me as a child" and "Let your heart stay on me, it might look all shaky around but hang in there, don't settle for cheap alternatives, and I will come through for you."

Trust, faith. Two words, one meaning, capable of changing our lives for the better or worse, depending on how we use it or how it's used in relation to us. He wants us to trust Him because His love has and can be proven.

> *Proverbs 3: 5-6(MSG): "Trust God from the bottom of your heart; don't try to figure out everything on your own. Listen for God's voice in everything you do, everywhere you go; he's the one who will keep you on track."*

Love "Hangs Out"

D o you have a friend or group of friends that you get along well with? Someone or people you feel get you? I mean, you're able to be yourself around them. They know you drool, snore, are rubbish at expressing yourself, and so on and yet, they put up with you and, of course, vice versa.

Just like us, God likes to "hang out" with us, and like our besties, He's cool with us. This is because He knows us. He likes to hang out with us by talking to Him when we pray, keeping ourselves and making time for Him when we fast, and listening to Him as we live in His name. When we hang out with our friends, it's not a one-way conversation, God speaks too, and yes, sometimes it's a lot and sometimes not so much, but He speaks. Like when you meet a new friend, you don't just blurt out everything. As friends get to know one another better with time, you come to understand and deepen the relationship over time.

When we spend time with people in our social circle, there is joy in being together. The catch-ups, gossips, pouring out, support, and shared experiences. The feeling of this is so right. Just like us, God loves it when we spend time with Him, and we both leave enriched by the conversations we've had.

Ecclesiastes 4: 9(MSG): "It's better to have a partner than go it alone..."

Love Excites

o you remember the first time you fell in love or had your crush (whether in primary or high school or at any other time)? Do you remember how excited you were? The heartbeats that pounded when this person came into the room, the rush of butterflies in your stomach, the fumbled speech, the boundless joy, the limitless pleasure, the happy times together, the sneaky getaways, the sad goodbyes, the longings for the next appointments, the daydreaming, the sleepless nights, and countless other emotions.

As we grow up, we begin to know that many of these feelings are features of lust, not love, and while most of these early feelings fizzle out, we are aware of their power to shape our realities.

Undoubtedly, there is an exciting part of love, and if there is no excitement or "chemistry" as it's known, most likely it's not love. Love excites. Love takes you from where you are and dreams up incredible possibilities that fuel the passion for life.

God, who is love, is no different. More so, His love is selfless. A relationship with God is exciting, filled with the thrills and excitement that are unparalleled.

* * *

Technology is amazing! Technological innovations help illustrate how the unseen and the unknown can still impact what we see and know. Through the ages and decades, we've been able to do countless things that were probably never thought possible at one time. Of course, life is a lot more convenient than it has been, and with Artificial Intelligence, driver less cars, and robotics, the possible permutations are vast. Our connectivity through Wi-Fi, for example, is one we've grown accustomed to in the last few decades. Though we don't physically see the signals, devices such as our phones or laptops have been configured to detect them effortlessly, pick them up, and translate them for our ease and use.

New and emerging technologies expose us to more excellent tools, insights, and secrets designed to simplify our lives (imagine the joy of people when washing machines were invented!). Just like the excitement of discovering something new, different, or better; our love relationship with God takes us on thrills the more we get to know Him. As we configure and fine-tune our spirits (device) to pick up the perfect signal (remember the era when the TV/radio signal had to be adjusted to align to the best frequency for clarity?), we move closer to the source (God) for uninterrupted signal. Here, the manifest presence of God (the Holy Spirit) shows and tells us things that only He can reveal, to address our issues, comforting and instructing us as He turns our lives around for

His glory.

Just as using technology requires a level of trust (which is why some choose not to use devices with digital transmissions, such as computers or phones), being in a love relationship with God requires trust. This can be daunting and yet exciting. There are so many "close your eyes" moments when we are invited to relinquish control, leave our perfectly planned future and trust Him completely. "Hold my hands," let me lead you, let me guide you and "open your eyes," see where I've brought you, you couldn't have done this by yourself surprise moments in store when we choose to walk with Him! And the incredible thing is, with God, there's no disappointment because He knows what He's doing. He has it all planned out—plans to take care of you, not abandon you, plans to give you the future you hope for and make your wildest dreams come true.

Love journeys with God have so many OMG moments. OMG, moments are times when we look back and see how He perfectly pieces every puzzle in our lives to form a picture that tells a story and makes us realize that He's been there all along, even in those times when it wasn't apparent. Just like us, experiencing His love is exciting, both for Him and for us.

Romans 8:15-17(MSG): "This resurrection life you received from God is not a timid, grave tending life. It's adventurously expectant, greeting God with a childlike 'What's next, Papa?' God's Spirit touches our spirits and confirms who we truly are."

Love Befriends

What impresses you the most about true friendship? Is it how well true friends know each other? Is it how they see past the charade and can provide support where it's needed? Is it how they can count on each other regardless of the storm? Or is it how they're able to bond again and become stronger through doubts and betrayal?

God has not only called us to be His lovers and children, but He's also called us to be His friends. The Bible describes on different occasions where God walked with us, humans—whether it was in the garden of Eden with Adam, with Abraham the Father of Faith, or with Enoch, who walked with God. Walking with someone we love creates an opportunity for dialogue, getting to know each other, getting angry, laughing together, getting to the same destination, and enjoying each moment. Our walk with God is designed to get us to know God and Him knowing us. And when I say "Him knowing us," I mean just that. Of course, God is sovereign and knows everything. But that's not the side we're exploring here.

Through examples in the Bible, we know that our Heavenly Father can be vulnerable, just like we are. Vulnerable, but not weak. Vulnerable because love does that to us. He seeks to know us, to be able to rely on us, to trust us, to be boastfully proud of us. An example that we can see is the story of Job, where He called out Job as an exemplar friend (Job 1:8 Message Bible).

In His call for us to walk with Him, God wants to deepen our knowledge of Him and vice versa. Just like our closest friends know our intimate secrets, He wants to trust us with His secrets. He wants to open our eyes to depths unimaginable. He wants to deepen our insights and reveal what we could otherwise have missed. That's how Daniel, in the Bible, for example, excelled. He reviewed God and responded to His "friend" request. He "followed" Him, digesting every one of His "posts" on His social media channel (the Bible). He relied on His Spirit to enlighten Him on His ways, and just as every social media account owner knows, "likes" are great, but "comments" are better. A "like" in this context could be going to church but not living a Christ-centric life. "Comments" here would mean reading His "post," understanding (meditating) on His post, and applying His post to our context enough to generate a "comment" that shows a deeper level of engagement with Him.

The Bible talks about ministering angels (His social media content manager(s)) who are "ministering" or "posting," ensuring His will/purpose is fulfilled on earth. So, you know when you've posted that video on Facebook/ YouTube/ Instagram, and you're checking hour by hour or less extremely day by day to see the view counts? That's the same way our Heavenly Father and His angels are constantly checking. Did he read the post? Did she like it? Any comments? How many views? How many likes? How many comments? And of course, the golden question "Is it viral?" and viral for Him would be "How many people are doing what He's perfectly planned for them to do so they can obtain perfect results to live an amazingly awesome life?"

Unlike social media "friends" and followers where the "star/account holder" doesn't know their friends/followers on a personal level, our God does. The Bible says He knows our name. We are inscribed (tattooed—OMG!) on the palm of His hands. He doesn't want us to live empty lives and not have a future with Him on the streets of gold post transit from our mortal bodies (death), and it's not just a promise for the future; it encapsulates living the fullest life now. A life of peace, a life of joy, a life of insight, a life of direction, and ultimately, an adventurous and exciting life as we rely on Him.

God's call for friendship is a call for intimacy. One where He delights in us and we in Him. One where we are embraced in the warmth of His love, one where we are secure in the assurance of His dependability, one that encompasses everything and more that we would like or already have in a friend indeed.

Proverbs 17:17(MSG): "Friends love through all kinds of weather, and families stick together in all kinds of trouble."

Love Relives

ny group of people with shared experiences know how it feels to relive past times. For example, a couple may be moving through a rough patch in their marriage. Trying to remember and relive how they got together, what feelings they had then, what made them choose each other, helps rekindle a close bond that strengthens their relationship. Likewise, families, friends, and colleagues, when reliving past experiences, especially the good ones, will know that reentering is an invaluable tool to reconnect.

Reliving our best experiences helps to put things into perspective, helps us to be grateful, helps strengthen our bond. It's a feeling of life and love.

Just like us, our Heavenly Father relives our times with Him and it strengthens our bond. God told the Israelites as they were about to enter the promised land to relive their deliverance from Egypt's experience, to remind them of His love affair with them. How they met and started on their love journey and how refreshing it was to have Him in their lives. God also relives His love affair when He talks about how He picked up Israel as a baby, how He washed them, cared for them, how they entered puberty over His watchful eyes and so on.

Reminiscing on His love for us may take simple playbacks on how we won the race to be born in the first place, with millions of competitors at our conception. It may be how, in the most challenging times, we've come through stronger and better. It may be times when there was a miracle that turned things around at the point of giving up. It may be passing an exam that we had at one time been convinced was going to be a failure. It may be getting a job we didn't even interview for.

Like us, He relives his shared experience with us, and when we do this with Him or our loved ones, we indeed feel more connected and strengthened in our relationship.

Ezekiel 16: 11-13(MSG): "...I adorned you with jewelry: I placed bracelets on your wrists, fitted you out with a necklace, emerald rings, sapphire earrings, and a diamond tiara. You were provided with everything precious and beautiful: with exquisite clothes and elegant food, garnished with honey and oil. You were absolutely stunning. You were a queen!..."

Love Completes

D o you remember when you fell in love and didn't want to be with anyone else? You felt complete, and with this person, you really could face whatever came your way.

Remember the joy that emanated from your inside when you realized you or your spouse was pregnant? Regardless of the external circumstance, whether it was the worry of not knowing how you would provide for the little one or that there was no partner with you on the journey or that you had everything required and were so ready on every side or anything else, you felt complete. Love has the power to complete, and it's not about being perfect; it's the awareness that there is no vacuum on the inside of you, the feeling of knowing that all will be well.

Just like us, God feels complete when He has us in His life. That's why when we're in a healthy relationship with Him (note that this is not religion), which we know is not about obeying a set of commands which one gets penalized for breaking at every opportunity but following a set of conducts that protects our union, nurtures our love and creates an environment where we can develop, grow and protects our values. In a healthy relationship with God, completeness is enacted on God's side and our side. Regardless of who we are or where we are in our life's journey, God's love will meet and complete us, like a lover completes his loved one and vice versa. It leaves no room for a vacuum. It's exhilarating and perfect.

Colossians 2:10(MSG): "When you come to him, that fullness comes together for you, too. His power extends over everything."

Love Disciplines

⚜

The importance of rewards and consequences cannot be overemphasized in raising well-balanced children. Ultimately, the choice is given to the child with instructions well laid out to help understand the implications of their decisions. Then, out of love, a parent ensures that the rewards and consequences are followed through, even if the child throws a tantrum and tries to have their way. By following through, the child learns and emerges as a balanced child, a balanced learner, and a balanced person, contributing to the broader society balance.

God's love allows for discipline, allowing better versions of us to emerge. Just like parents have consequences for disobedience, God has consequences for disobedience, with the ultimate goal of setting us on the straight and narrow. And please don't confuse God's discipline with concepts widely discussed regarding sicknesses, diseases, and poverty being God's hallmark of asserting authority. The gospel of our Lord Jesus does not validate this. Instead, Jesus healed everyone he came in contact with (Acts 10:38). Surely this contradicts these beliefs, and the Bible has to be the standard here. God's discipline, just like ours, is training that will result in better shaping.

Proverbs 3: 11-12(MSG): "But don't, dear friend, resent God's discipline; don't sulk under His loving correction. It's the child he loves that God corrects; a father's delight is behind all this."

Love Sings

⁓◦◦◦⁓

A child was only a few months old. She was crying, upset by what was seemingly unclear to her mother. She wasn't hungry. It was not napping time. She wasn't wet, hot, or cold. After trying a few things here and there that made no difference, her mother began to sing. At first, it made little difference to the child, but as her mother continued slowly, the loud cries softened to low-pitched cooing until she stopped crying altogether. *"Victory!"* Her mother thought.

What do you feel when you sing? Now add a few or more dance moves to it, and now what do you feel? I still haven't figured it out yet, but something about music goes from the words we speak in a tune through our thoughts and emotions to our innermost self.

Have you observed how music in high demand is usually about love? Broken hearts, new love, failing love, something love. Do you wonder why we all respond to music and lyrics? How do we distinguish a song from the heart from a song on the lips?

Just like us, God sings and His song, of course—you guessed it!—revolves around His love for us, which Zephaniah 3:17 precisely captures. Here the Bible describes how, underpinned by love, God rejoices over us with singing! So, next time your singing reminds you of a loved one, or you sing for a loved one, know He actively sings for you, too!

Zephaniah 3:17(MSG): "Jerusalem will be told: 'Don't be afraid. Dear Zion, don't despair. Your God is present among you, a strong Warrior there to save you (my knight in shining armour :))*. Happy to have you back, he'll calm you with his love and delight you with his songs.'"*

Love is Authentic

I love romantic movies. I love watching how love triumphs. I see how God tries to win our love in these movies. I recently watched a movie on Netflix and was reminded of how analogous our love affair with God is. In this movie, there was a guy who had been heartbroken by the one person he deeply loved. Since then, he couldn't commit to anyone else. He was privileged, handsome, and wealthy, and because of this, he had people who constantly threw themselves at him. Then, one night, he met a dancer who wasn't the norm. She expressed herself where others had not questioned him. She also didn't use her body to gratify his sexual needs and was quite open and honest about her feelings. As a result, he saw her true self. This was intriguing for him because he was used to the complete opposite. Everyone wanted to use him for what he could offer to meet their needs, so they faked it relentlessly around him, but she was different. In sum, he fell in love with her and won her heart eventually, with a happy ending.

I'm reminded of God in this guy. Just like him, God's heart was broken when Adam gave Him up at the garden of Eden. Since then, He tried to fill the love vacuum for man, and He's had so many people follow him with their mouths but not their hearts. I'm sure, as humans, we know the difference between the two. The Pharisees and Sadducees in the time of Jesus were examples of this. They used God for their gains. Outwardly, they said yes to Him, deceiving others, but they were not sold to Him the way true lovers are but instead were motivated by fame, greed, and wealth.

Like this girl that stole the guy's heart, God is looking for people who are true to themselves, genuine, sincere, not deceptive, not manipulative, not liars. He wants people whom He can genuinely win over because their heart is right. He wants people who are not trying to use Him as a means to an end but as an end in itself. People with no ulterior motives or hidden agendas, just true lovers as love should be. David in the Bible was one example of this. He loved God. His heart was always with God, and that's not to say he was perfect because we're not designed to be perfect, but he was sincere.

Just like the guy in the movie who ended up wooing and marrying that woman—someone who wanted him for who he was rather than what he could give, God wants authentic lovers He can commit Himself to. Ones who love Him, just like He loves them, ones He will share His everything with, and with God, everything, is indeed everything!

> *Matthew 15:8-9(MSG): "These people make a big show of saying the right thing, but their heart isn't in it. They act like they're worshipping me, but they don't mean it. They just use me as a cover for teaching whatever suits their fancy."*

Love Yields

❧

I t started with a question, one that came from a parent. It was at a marriage ceremony, and the wine had run out.

"But mum," He said, "it's not yet time."

His mum went to the servers and told them, "Do what He tells you."

I didn't expect Him to respond because He already said it wasn't time. But, interestingly, he gave the instruction that changed the outcome for all persons present at the party, making it a merrier time because He provided the best.

This is the story of the first miracle of Jesus in the Bible. His first response indicated He was not prepared for the giant leap, the bold step into something new, something unusual, something uncertain, something different. Finally, however, He yielded to His mother's instructions. Interestingly, the Bible records this as His first miracle because I think it has significance. Why did He have to be prompted? Why did He say He was not ready? Why did He respond to His mother's instruction to the servers?

In life, we all get prompted, sometimes from the inside, sometimes from external sources. When these promptings come, just like Jesus, we retract, tell ourselves it is not going to work, give ourselves reasons why it would fail and get discouraged, even before we start.

This example shows us the humanity in Jesus. He was *just like us*, and like so many of us who have pushed through the hardships, the pain, the shame, and so many other boundaries that exist to prevent us from experiencing our first miracle. Yet, he shows us that by yielding to His love for His mother, He was able to turn a party that would have been a disgrace to the bride and groom into a graceful celebration of love and satisfaction. In addition, he was able to improve the experience of everyone at the occasion by providing the most "exquisite" wine, as per the words of the chairman of the occasion, a man that would have been well versed in wine tasting.

Sometimes, the gulf seems too broad between us and what we have been equipped to do. The voices in our heads speak damnation to discourage us even before starting. The circumstances around us tell us we will not make it, and just like us, He experienced that. Remarkably, the story didn't end there because He yielded to love. And so will we. We will yield to the love of our Heavenly Father, yield to His voice within us, turn things around for the better and be prepared to launch into the world of "miracles," no matter how big or small. We will yield to doing good that will positively impact our world. We will yield to making a lasting positive change. We will yield to making a difference that matters.

1 Thessalonians 5:24(MSG): "The One who called you is completely dependable. If he said it, he'd do it!"

Love is Dogged

◦━━⟨✦⟩━━◦

It was time for her shower. She hurried into the bathroom and locked the door behind her. Taking a deep breath, she was glad she had a 15–20 mins escape. Having a three-year-old, the pandemic and resulting lockdown had increased her toddler's attachment to her. With words like "I want mummy," "Where's mummy?" "Mummy!" sounding all day and juggling work with family within the four walls of a building that's not exactly big; it was mostly good but sometimes challenging.

Five minutes into the shower, the door started pounding,"Mummy!". With the shower water running and knowing that other household members were around who had offered assistance, this an attachment issue that had to be addressed. Continuing her shower and hoping the toddler on the other side of the door would learn to be less needy, she continued to shower. The pounding continued and continued. It was clear this toddler was not going to give up, so she had to give up the shower.

Love is dogged, determined, and persistent. This toddler refused to give up in her quest to secure her mother's attention. Just like us, God's unending love continues to be on the lookout for us. Whether it's in small moments of wonder or big moments where things could have gone awry, like missing a fatal crash and so on, he continues to chase us, hoping we would respond to Him.

It doesn't matter where you are in your journey with Him. Whether you've yet to respond to His love proposal, or you've already made Him the center of your existence, He's still dogged in seeking you, still interested in spending time with you, still savoring your affection, still captivated by your attention.

He loves you, and it does not matter how many times He has to knock (Rev 3:20) to be given an audience. He is dogged and will never give up on the chance to woo you into a continuous personal relationship with Him.

Romans 8: 38-39(MSG): "...I'm convinced that nothing—nothing living or dead, angelic or demonic, today or tomorrow, high or low, thinkable or unthinkable—absolutely nothing can get between us and God's love because of the way that Jesus our Master has embraced us."

Love is Proactive

 ᢙᠬᡦᠣ

"I saw this and thought you might like it…." Receiving a thoughtful surprise gift from a loved one, whether a spouse, child, or friend, usually elicits a positive emotion. The pro-activeness of love makes you think of the person the gift is being bought for. What they like and how you could enhance their life in however small or large way. Sometimes we do this just to see the surprise on their face, watching the smile break out. Sometimes it's the tears and maybe the hug. Love always seeks ways to please, to make happy, and to fulfill.

Like us, our Heavenly Father seeks to please, make us happy, and fulfill us proactively. The Bible talks about God loving us while we were unaware of Him, sending Jesus to redeem us to His side. This gift of salvation is the most precious gift of all. While it may not look to mean much on the outside, the transformation inside is an overwhelming gift of completeness that touches every sphere of our being, our physical, mental, emotional, and spiritual self.

Sadly, as we know, not all surprise gifts elicit the desired response. What if the gift is; not opened? sneered at? disregarded? or met with ingratitude?. In this same vein, our Heavenly Father has experienced these same feelings over and over, with people rejecting His offer of love, acceptance, and care over and over again.

Just like us, He is heartbroken by this, and like a lover committed to wooing his bride, He always tries another way again.

Jeremiah 31:3(MSG): "....met God out looking for them! God told them, 'I've never quit loving you and never will. Expect love, love, and more love!"

Love is Patient

⁓꒰꒱⁓

L ove is patient. It's not uneasily compelling; it's not interested in unsubstantiated cheap thrills that leaves the other person with "the-morning-after" dilemma.

Just like us, when there is true love and not lust or infatuation, God is patient. He is patient to wait for us. He is patient to check out how we're feeling. He is patient for us to call Him. He is patient when we don't feel like socializing with Him (praying). Just like a young man, crazily in love with a lady he has asked out, waiting for an answer, God wants to throw Himself at us. He wants to show us His glory, His mysteries. He wants to take us on the ride of our lives and show us His love as real as the air we breathe. He wants to envelop us in His affection but knowing it's a relationship where the feelings of both parties matter, He waits…

Imagine the lover on a rollercoaster ride of loving emotions and the loved, static/walking. The lover here presses the breaks, pauses, and waits to get to the motion level of the loved. It's different for the lover but knowing the importance of "together," He knows it's a sacrifice that would embed trust at the epicenter of their relationship. One that would be useful in their journey for years, possibly decades to come. Love is patient…

1 Corinthians 13:4(TPT): "Love is large and incredibly patient. Love is gentle and consistently kind to all. It refuses to be jealous when a blessing comes to someone else. Love does not brag about one's achievements nor inflate its importance."

Love is Multi-Faceted

Every individual is multi-dimensional. A woman, for instance, can have all these roles: daughter, sister, wife, mother, friend, employee, colleague, neighbor, mentor, mentee and so on and the role determines the characteristics displayed. For instance, the prime minister of New Zealand is also a mother, a wife, etc. In the office, she is the prime minister, and she conducts herself in that manner. At home, she is a mum, and her daughter probably asks her to crawl on her knees as she climbs on her for a horse-riding session.

Just like us, God is multi-faceted. He is a creator, a judge, a defender, a protector, a provider, a lover, a father, and so on. God's multiple facets allow Him to express Himself in different ways to different people at different times.

His multi-faceted nature allows us to access the version of Him that speaks to our situation, whether a healer (Jehovah Rapha) if it's a sickness holding us bound. Whether a provider (Jehovah Jireh) for when we're in need, whether it's purity or righteousness (Jehovah Tsidkenu), whether it's God being there (Jehovah Shammah) and so on. He is one

God, and He can be many things to us and still be the same, just like us.

> *Psalm 18:1-2(TLB): "Lord, how I love you! For you have done such tremendous things for me. The Lord is my fort where I can enter and be safe; no one can follow me in and slay me. He is a rugged mountain where I hide; he is my saviour, a rock where none can reach me, and a tower of safety. He is my shield. He is like the strong horn of a mighty fighting bull."*

Love is Content

Have you heard the saying that money cannot buy love? And yes, this is not discrediting money or its immense value, but really, money cannot buy love in terms of its intricate, contented, joyful workings from inside out.

This is why someone may give up their well-paid income and exotic living to do something that they are passionate about. Despite offering a lower financial return, such a person doesn't mind because the initial lifestyle attempted to camouflage the inner lack of contentment. However, when the switch is made, the discontentment is replaced by contentment, a proof of love.

Also, that's why people will give up the throne to be with the person they are fulfilled with. That's why the wealthiest people are not necessarily the happiest, and that's why people who appear materially poor may have the best quality of life possible because there is love. Even in that "poverty," the deep contentment experienced leads to joy, not the happiness that materialism offers.

Just like us, God's love for us is content. That's why it doesn't matter who we are, where we've been, or what we've done. Once we accept Him as the Lord of our lives, He is content with us. And of course, just like being content doesn't mean complacency or lack of zest to make things better, financially, or otherwise, God's contentment with us accepts us as we are and, at the same time, works with us to bring us to where we would be truly comfortable. Note that this may not be instantaneous; it may take time and what is sure is that He is with us all the way, working out everything for our good.

Love's contentment gives the inner peace and joy that makes us stop striving—striving for a man's approval, being noticed, being heard, striving to make a mark. And this is not saying that these things are not good. However, the notable keyword here is "striving," which involves a laborious exertion that leaves its victims motivated by the wrong reasons, ending up exhausted. With God's love, contentment starts with knowing who you are in God, knowing you're the apple of His eye, knowing He gave up His best to be with you, to be loved by you. This starts you off contented, knowing that regardless of what's going on around you, He's got you, as a loving father, a lover, and a friend.It makes you know that you have the best there ever is, His love, which cannot be compared or traded with.

This standpoint is empowering because as you lean on His love for you and spend time knowing Him and Him knowing you, you discover His great plans that are unique for your person, your gifts, talent, experiences, etc. This will make you stand out and eventually stand tall.

Love's contentment stabilizes you in the moment of shaking, sometimes when it seems like all is lost, sometimes when it feels like there is no way forward. You remember Him and know that regardless of the challenges, you're not alone, and as you lean in on Him, you start to get directions on what to do and how to do it, which turns things around.

There is a story of a woman who didn't have anything to eat with her children, and she leaned in on God's love to understand what to do in that dire situation. She felt prompted to go to the supermarket and get a trolley without a penny in her bag. She felt prompted to pick everything she needed, and though she felt crazy, she obeyed the prompting. She filled up the trolley and went to the checkout, and of course, she still didn't know how she would pay. When it was her turn to be served, there was an announcement in the shop that everyone being served would have their shopping paid for by the supermarket as it was their opening anniversary. Imagine her delight. Imagine the silence the "other" voices knocking her would have gotten. It's unbelievable that that would have happened at that time.

Love's contentment allows peace despite turbulent circumstances and provides the foundation needed to achieve the extraordinary.

2 Corinthians 12:9(AMP): "...My grace is sufficient for you [My loving kindness and My mercy are more than enough – always available – regardless of the situation]; for [My] power is being perfected [and is completed and shows itself most effectively] in [your] weakness."

Love is Freedom

W hat does freedom mean, and are we truly free as humans? And this question is not about fights for justice that have created sensational shifts and have made those things that would have otherwise been unattainable within reach, for example, female voting, etc. These have changed how we operate as a society for good, that's for sure.

What is being referred here is freedom within ourselves, not external freedom. So, how free are we? There is a joke about giving people a choice, provided it is A or B. In this example, the choice is pre-determined, A or B.

I sometimes feel like that's how life is. Take media, for example. The information we are fed with most likely conditions us to take the actions that we take, which may not necessarily be correct. Tobacco, for instance, in the early 20th century, was promoted as being good. People were conditioned to smoke, there was societal pressure around it, and it was cool to be a smoker. But, of course, we now know in the 21st century that attitudes to smoking have changed considerably from this initial stance. So, when we examine choice/freedom in this context, are people free?

Examining love in the context of freedom, think about when you started dating. You were very careful to show and augment your perfect side to be acceptable to your partner (most likely if you liked this person). Then, as the relationship progressed, you got to a place where you felt free enough not to worry about if you looked good enough, I mean you could fart without being embarrassed! who would have thought that?!, nod off without fearing the dripping saliva and all the quirky, "Yes I know I'm weird" thoughts you have—all those sides that were carefully concealed initially.

True love allows you to be free. Over time, it allows you to be yourself, and it doesn't mean these traits don't annoy the other, but you know it's part of your love affair and forms your unique relationship.

Some people are cautious or not interested in accepting Jesus as their Lord and Savior because there is the fear that they will miss out, not be cool, have Him in control of their freedom and choice, etc., but in reality, this is so not true.

Being in a love relationship with God, through the finished work of Jesus and the presence of the Holy Spirit, allows you true freedom. Freedom to be yourself, freedom to have your real identity defined that is not tainted by the limitations or expectations of men for you. One that gives you confidence like no other, one that makes you secure in the knowledge of who you are in Him, one that truly sets you free.

Galatians 3: 13-15(MSG): "It is absolutely clear that God has called you to a free life. Just make sure that you don't use this freedom as an excuse to do whatever you want to do and destroy your freedom. Rather, use your freedom to serve one another in love; that's how freedom grows. For everything we know about God's Word is summed up in a single sentence: Love others as you love yourself. That's an act of true freedom...."

Love is Classic

⚜

They met purely by accident. They didn't like each other—at least initially—but they started spending time together by some coincidence. Their friendship grew, and so did their shared love. He proposed but was unsure of what her response would be. Her heart missed a beat when he looked at her. His gaze lingered just long enough when he looked at her; he couldn't get her out of his head. Now that he had proposed, he awaited the answer.

She couldn't believe this was happening; they got along well. With him, there was nothing forced, just natural. She didn't feel pressured in any way. She could be herself and relax. She enjoyed his company, and even though she had other suitors, she knew he was the one. The proposal was what she'd been waiting for, and of course, she said, "Yes!"

A classic love story, right? True, only this isn't just true for humans. Just like us, all through our lives, our ultimate lover tries to get our attention, tries to get us to care about Him, waits at the door, waiting to be invited in. Most believers will remember when they got saved, just as a lady remembers when she was proposed to. Though it may not look like it on the outside, getting saved is a big deal, and it's the only occasion recorded when an actual party happens in heaven.

Just like us, when a proposal is made and received, there is joy when a decision is made for Christ. It's synonymous with a wedding ceremony when we choose this one. He promises to love and keep, have and hold, protect and care for and in this relationship with Him, we do the same.

The salvation moment is a significant one and should be treated as such. Make a big deal of it, and please be proud. There's a party happening just for you! Enjoy that moment when you decide for Him.

1 John 3:1(NIV): "See what great love the Father has lavished on us, that we should be called children of God!"

Love is Companionship

✦

Have you ever wondered why we are created in families? Humans and animals alike. I know it is a bit of an odd question because that's the only model we know, but I don't think this could have been the only way. Families are important, families are our world, families help ground us, and of course, I know families can be irritating.

God created us for companionship. He created us to be with us, to live with us, and be His family. As humans, we're driven toward certain qualities that we find attractive in potential mates. God is attracted to us all regardless of our background, our social strata, and our history. We all meet His specifications. He made us in our different forms and personalities because He doesn't want to be bored. I guess we excite Him that way as He doesn't know what's coming from us on the side of Him we're exploring. The Bible is full of examples of different people who came to a knowledge of His love.

1 John 1:3-4(MSG): "We saw it, we heard it, and now we're telling

54

you so you can experience it along with us, this experience of communion with the Father and his Son, Jesus Christ. Our motive for writing is simply this: We want you to enjoy this, too. Your joy will double our joy!"

Love is Mutual

❧

She knows he loves her. He's done everything humanly possible to show it. Her friends and family have noticed it and advised her to consider this respectable gentleman who wouldn't break her heart, but she isn't budging. She has a thing for bad boys, and she isn't ready to give it up for this calm and collected guy.

Oh! I can't do this anymore. She doesn't like me, and I deserve better. It's such a shame, though. I would have been thrilled to have her. Okay. That's it. I need to move on. I have moved on.

Broken heart again! She is streaming tears, evaluating life; she realizes she was stupid, not choosing calm and certainty for upheaval and uncertainty. *I wonder if I still have a shot with him after all this time and how I've treated him.* She shows up at his door, wanting to re-ignite his old affection for her. Knock, knock. The door opens, and it's his fiancée, stunningly beautiful. Coming right behind her, he shows up. She knows it's too late; he's glad it's too late.

You didn't choose me when you could. I'm not a last resort, an "if nothing else works, then this should." I'm a person with feelings, and I deserve to be with someone who prioritizes me and wants to be with me as their first choice.

Unpleasantly surprised and sad, she goes home. She's lost the opportunity to be with the one person who truly loved her. It is painful, it is sad, it is late. Too late.

* * *

I love science and technology. I think that quite often, science demonstrates the existence of God. Let's explore one aspect of this very quickly. In science, the law of thermodynamics states that energy can neither be created nor destroyed only changed from one form to another. Using this law, I'd like to explain the concept of terminal living and eternal life. As humans, we have a physical body, which is the medium by which we're allowed to live on earth. But, in addition, we have a soul, the seat of our intellect, emotions, etc., and something else (called spirit). The spirit part of life, the eternal part of life, can only live in this world because the body houses it. When the body can no longer sustain one's spirit, either through sickness, disease, accident, etc., terminal living ends; however, eternal living continues, which is where the concept of eternal life stems from.

God's creation of humans in the Bible is made possible by using the elements of the earth. As it is written (Gen 2:7), "the Lord God formed man out of the clay of the ground and blew into his nostrils the breath of life, and man became a living being." The term Eden is derived from the Sumerian word *Eden,* which means fertile plain. Phosphorus, magnesium, calcium, selenium, name it, a good number of the periodic-table elements that exist in nature are also how our physical bodies survive and thrive. It's where healthy eating for good health and longevity stems from and points to. It's why mechanically derived foods from processing do the most damage to our bodies because they are not found naturally in nature and the earth, the origin of our bodies.

When God formed man from dust, He then said to make man in His image and after His likeness, which "Just Like Me" elaborates on. Then, in the second part of man's formation, He breathes into man. This breath is what gave man life, eternal life, like God. That is why a body without the spirit is commonly said to be lifeless, so I'm sure you've heard the expression "lifeless body," "the body lay lifeless," etc. because just as a container houses a specific type of content, so does the body house our spirit.

The thermodynamics law states that energy is neither created nor destroyed but transformed from one form to another. Here, we can see that man's "creation" was a transformation from soil to body and God's spirit to man's spirit. While soil and body may look different, they have the same rudimentary composition, and while God's life and man's life may not appear parallel, again, they are made from the same materials. There are potentially different ways to explore this, but let us focus on life after death. When a man dies, the body decomposes back to the soil and is re-used, some of the practical examples of the law of thermodynamics. In the same manner, the unceasing life of God is taken back to its source, like the minerals to earth.

It may seem like we have complete control of our lives whilst we still possess a viable host, aka the human body, however, the moment of death transitions this autonomy. As we know, years of eating unhealthily results in diseases that can lead to untimely cessation of physical existence. Conversely, a healthy approach to living is likely to yield dividends of longevity and good health. Actions lead to inevitable consequences; there are cause-and-effect repercussions in our relationships with our real "life" as well. For example, a life spent dishonoring or not acknowledging God has the grievous effect of missing out on eternal life with God.

If we take a look at chemical reactions as an analogy, there are reversible and irreversible ones. As the name suggests, reversible reactions are ones where the reactants can change to the product, and the products can change back to the reactants—practical examples such as ice melting into water. If the water is subject to freezing temperature, it converts back to ice. In irreversible reactions, it is impossible to get the reactants back once the product is formed in the chemical reaction. So, burning wood is an example here; fire and the substance burned cannot return to their original state after that process has been completed.

The trigger point to enter irreversibility with eternal "life" is death. After which point, like a burned item, there is no going back on the decisions that could have been made whilst still in the body.

Just like us, when we feel taken for granted, ignored, or abandoned, we move on, and there's a point where we can't go back. God's the same. All mortals have a chance to choose Him while we're still alive, to decide for Him, to prioritize Him. The chance is valid while we're still breathing in our mortal bodies, after which it will be too late to accept His love proposal.

Hebrews 9:27-28(MSG): "Everyone has to die once, then face the consequences. Christ's death was also a one-time event, but it was a sacrifice that took care of sins forever. And so, when he next appears, the outcome for those eager to greet him is, precisely, salvation."

Love is Jealous

Jealousy is a word we're familiar with, especially in a love relationship. When we feel like we're not getting enough of the love of our lives, whether it's their job, hobby, or worse, someone else competing for our lover's time, attention, and other scarce resources, we become jealous. We're angry and upset because this person we love is interested in someone or something else. We're not the center of their attention like they are ours, and it threatens our security and our trust with this person, making us feel less than we are.

Whether it's jealousy in its basic form or hypersensitive jealousy, which may be unhealthy, jealousy arises because there is a vested interest in that person that the "jealous" person doesn't feel is being reciprocated. It's like we're giving more than we're getting, and we feel cheated.

Jealousy won't be present if there is no emotional investment, and by that, I mean that if you don't care about someone, you can't be jealous of them, so jealousy is a sign of care, affection, and love, i.e., you're jealous about someone you have feelings for. Here, I'm referring to jealousy in its primary sense.

Just like us, God is a jealous God, a jealous lover, and He's jealous because He loves us. He's invested so much in having a relationship with us that it hurts Him when He's not the center of our focus. He's jealous of us because He wants us to be the best versions of ourselves, and just like a leaf is only green when still connected to the tree, we can only be "green," full of life, fulfilling our purpose (photosynthesis for the leaf) while connected to Him. Therefore, his jealousy over us is more advantageous to us than it is to Him (think of a fallen leaf vs being part of a tree with lots of leaves).

> *Deuteronomy 6: 13-15(MSG): "Deeply respect God, your God. Serve and worship him exclusively. Back up your promises with his name only. Don't fool around with other gods, the gods of your neighbors, because God, your God, who is alive among you, is a jealous God."*

Love has Faith

I used to wonder if faith was something only Christians or people of religion had to have. I mean, the concept of God who is not readily seen or heard goes against our natural senses, and I had this belief until it dawned on me that everyone has to live by faith. Everyone.

If we examine a couple saying their vows on their wedding day, they have to have faith that they will not evolve into a version that ends up in dissatisfaction or divorce. A woman has faith that when she gets pregnant, her child will be healthy. An employer has faith that the person given the opportunity to join their organization will be a good fit. We make phone calls and say, "see you tomorrow" by faith. We drive our cars having faith that we will arrive at our destination safely. We eat, having faith that that food doesn't contain substances harmful to our bodies. These are some of the most mundane things in life, things we take for granted, but all and many more, carried out by faith, and it doesn't end there.

Some of the most audacious innovations in our existence have been based solely on faith! The Wright brothers, best known for their contribution to the aviation industry, pioneered the first successful aeroplane when there was nothing like it. It was by faith. Another word for faith in conventional living is the power of walking a vision through to completion. It entails believing the endpoint, goal or objective before it is entirely plausible and taking the necessary steps through to what success looks like. Every inventor knows that they first envisioned the invention in their minds before it was manufactured. Every successful organization leader knows they first saw their organization thrive in their niche, and so on.

So, when I think about it again, faith is part of who we are. It's what makes us humans or maybe even mammals. It's what has made us evolve from primitive beings to the sophistication we now enjoy.

Faith in God, faith in yourself, faith in your business, faith in your spouse, faith in your child(ren) are all expressions of who we are. I think it's impossible to be human without it. Why then is faith in God often seen as something ludicrous or unimaginable? Without faith in God, there already is an alternative model to which we're subscribed, whether we like it or not. Just like a computer software comes pre-configured, not choosing your customizations doesn't mean it won't have any; it only means you go with the default.

Without actively customizing our lives by accepting Jesus as their Lord and Savior, many humans have already set themselves to the default human mode, being led by self (or the king of this world). This means that there is little room for expressing your true self as you strive to look like everyone else. Doing what everyone else is doing in the default mode that everyone else operates in is tragic. Especially when there is that inner knowing deep down that there is room for "customizations" or more because, in God, we don't just go through motions but get to live life richly and uniquely; Jesus said He came so that we may experience living the way it was intended when we trust in God, an abundant life.

Have you ever had a situation where you bought a gadget or something and only used its most basic function? You've gone through a lot of hassle because of your lack of knowledge of this device. So, the day you find out how more the gadget could offer to make your life easier, you're like, "OMG, I didn't know it could do that!?" This often happens with cars, phones, etc. It's the same with us! When we allow God to take us through His manual for our lives, we experience so much more enrichment, so much more life.

Just like us, God has faith. When He created man, He had faith that we would choose Him. That's why we were ever made. He had faith in us when He made sure that we were born and are still alive despite everything. He had faith when He sent His son to die for our sins. He still has faith in humanity. That's why our world still exists.

> *Hebrews 11:6(MSG): "It's impossible to please God apart from faith. And why? Because anyone who wants to approach God must believe both that he exists and that he cares enough to respond to those who seek him."*

Love is Loyal

H ave you ever felt the sting of betrayal? The rush of negative emotions, the disbelief initially, and then gradually summing up of all the tell-tale signs that disjointly didn't mean much, then the feeling of being used, sometimes the hopeless feeling of "where do I go from here after all we've been through?!" Whether it's the betrayal of a spouse, friend, or child, the feeling that wells up on the inside is definitely not love because love is loyal.

Just like us, God does feel betrayed. He's had (and most likely having) the feeling of His heart ripped out and, yes, by us humans. The Bible book of Hosea (13;4-6) tells us how God's first love, the Israelites, always cheated on him at every available opportunity and expresses the pain He went through. The story of God's feelings about the infidelity of humans with Him is spread across the Bible, and He talks about how much of Himself He gave in the hard times, the years there was nothing and how He took care of all their needs, gave them everything they needed. Yet they forgot Him by going off to worship other gods (God here is anything that takes the center of our lives that isn't God, so family, work, wealth, etc.). God remembers how He lifted the Israelites as a baby to His cheek, how He bent down to feed them, and how He simply doesn't understand why they would choose to leave Him, and He can't bear His desolation as they've left Him. He was heartbroken, just like us when betrayed.

No one likes to be taken advantage of, and love does not take advantage. It is not deceptive; it does not trick; it does not leave the other person feeling cheated.

Whether you decide to move on or forgive in your instance, one thing God and us can agree on is that betrayal is awful and does not feel good at all.

Lamentations 3:22-24(MSG): "God's loyal love couldn't have run out, his merciful love couldn't have dried up. They're created new every morning. How great your faithfulness! I'm sticking with God (I say it over and over). He's all I've got left."

Love Praises

T hink about it for a second; there is something extraordinary about praise. When you receive praise, the feeling is always a good one. It changes perspective. Whether it's the simple "well done," "good job," "awesome," "great," or the more in-depth "This is good because...," being praised takes us to a place of joy, a place of contentment and a place of peace. Praise feels satisfactory.

Just like us, God loves to be praised. He likes us to show gratitude. He likes us to acknowledge Him. He loves praise so much that the Bible talks about Him dwelling in the praises of His people (Psalms 22:3). That's how much He loves it.

Praise stems from gratitude and gratitude from appreciation. Just like us, our Heavenly Father loves it.

> *Psalms 22:3(DAR): "And thou art holy, thou that dwellest amid the praises of Israel."*

Love Cries

T he parent remembers saying, "the oven tray is very hot, don't go near it." But recalcitrant, the child touches it anyway. Everything spirals very quickly. Infected, the finger has to be amputated to save the life of the child.

When the mother is told, she breaks down in tears, weeping inconsolably, thinking about how the child will not feel the completeness of that hand, how people will treat and possibly make fun of him. He's only just begun his life, yet he is going to be prejudiced against. And here she was, unable to help, shattered, heartbroken, and deeply sad because the child made that choice.

There could be many questions about why this happened in the first place. For example, why was the tray within reach? Why was the boy not tended to? This fictional example is easily replaceable with happenings with similar outcomes, such as a teenage car crash with fatal consequences, a daughter's relationship with a lad we can't exactly vouch for, and so on. As parents, we know things happen, and this was where this family was.

For a lover just like me, it's hard not to say that our Heavenly Father cries. There is no definitive account of that in the Bible, but Jesus was recorded to have wept, and God is recorded to laugh, so He must also cry, right?

As an early Christian, I used to think that God didn't have any problems. You know, He's not mortal like me; He could literally do what He wants, and whilst that's true, however, because He's a just and righteous God with principles in place, even He has to follow the ordinated systems, despite creating them. Taking you back to A level biology, the human body comprises of systems such as digestive system, respiratory system, etc. that ensure that the body functions as designed. Disrupt one, and it's likely to impact the other. So, God created a system that allows man to dominate the earth and decide how it's run (*Psalm 115:16 - The highest heavens belong to the Lord, but the earth he has given to mankind*) that allows Him to *only* intervene when invited. In business, process maps show the system of business value delivery by illustrating how different teams interact with one another to achieve business objectives.

After I started to understand how much God loves us, sacrificing His son to redeem us, seeing how limited He was because of our lack of belief in Him, which could be synonymous to there being a block in the system such as if a person is unable to excrete or if a sales department does not bring in customers to the organization, causing disruption and a lack of flow. When I understood how our world reflects His world in different dimensions, I realized that uneasy lies the head that wears the crown indeed. I think God is going through a lot when all He wants is for His best to be accessible by us all.

Imagine what God goes through every time a person dies without knowing and accepting Him as their Lord and Savior because of unbelief. And this hurt and intense grief are not just because of unbelief in Him; it's more because it's irreversible after death, i.e., "Hell". Endless anguish, pain and torment.

Again, you may wonder why God doesn't stop this, and I'd like us to continue with the scenarios above where a person cannot excrete or when no customers are patronizing a business. In these cases, the systems in place make us understand that the outcome is death unless timely intervention is made. God, of course, tries His utmost to draw men unto Himself, but if we don't accept His intervention, then the system expression here is eternal death.

Life is more spiritual than physical, and that's why even in our usual, natural self, we know that some things just don't add up because what we see is not all there is.

Just like us, God weeps when we refuse to let Him come in and help us, come in and be the Lord of our lives, with the ultimate guarantee of eternal life, on the streets of gold, a place of beauty and rest. Take a look at nature, and indeed, there must be a witness within us that there is a higher being orchestrating all of this when we pause and ponder.

With us, while lots of things may make us weep, the loss of a loved one, the loss of a job, the hardness of a child's heart, lack of finances, etc., God weeps because of our unbelief, either as people who have not yet yielded to Him or as Christians who have not yielded completely. Just like us, feeling the agony and distress of what makes us weep, He does when we don't believe Him.

Mark 6:5–6(GW): "He couldn't work any miracles there except to lay his hands on a few sick people and cure them. Their unbelief amazed him."

John 11: 35(NIV): "Jesus wept"

Finally

G od has probably been portrayed as a killjoy—a being that doesn't allow fun, a being that stifles and inhibits you from being you. If that's what's holding you up from salvation, then nothing could be more untrue.

God is the author of everything good, and I'm just going to say it out loud, get ready for it: He created sex, and even better, He made it more meaningful in the context of love, acceptance, and marriage, where commitment and not heartbreak (for both guys and ladies) is the controlling force. As old as marriage as an institution is, it's still very fashionable regardless of how many knocks it has received in different ways over the centuries. Tell me about a girl/boy who has felt "used" and "dumped" by a so-called lover, and let's examine whose framework is better: God's framework for how love works or the alternative that breaks hearts, leaves people hardened, and creates adverse ripple/domino effects for all of us?

God approved of wine! That was his first miracle at the wedding, and it was described as the best wine by one of the most influential people in that setting. It probably would be termed "Bordeaux" or "exclusive" in current times, and I know some Christians who are opposed to drinking would disagree with this and think it's a license for people to get drunk. Yes, I know I don't drink any form of alcohol, and that's by choice, but honestly, it's black and white in the Bible. It's recorded as wine because it's wine (of course in moderation, as with anything!).

God isn't against abundant wealth; He loves it when His children are affluent. There was so much wealth and abundance in Solomon's time that silver was counted as nothing.

God isn't the enemy here; in Him is authentic living. He only wants everything used in the right way so that we don't use these tools to fulfill our selfish cravings to the detriment of others.

John 10: 10(MSG): "A thief is only there to steal and kill and destroy. I came so they can have real and eternal life, more and better life than they ever dreamed of."

Not Like Us

We're bound and limited by our frailties, and we are capped by our limitations. There's only so much we can do, and there's only so much we can give. We're not inexhaustible. We need to be replenished, and we need time to rejuvenate, aka, "Me Time." When a "'Me Time" is required, usually, nothing else matters, and that's fine because our bodies aren't designed to go for long periods without rest.

Unlike us, God is not bound by space and time. He doesn't grow old, tired, or weak. These are limitations imposed by our bodies, the operating system to live on earth, the same way your Microsoft Windows, Apple Mac OS, Apple iOS, Google Android, etc., allows you access to the world of computing. The Bible talks about Him not sleeping or slumbering as He watches over us, shielding us in moments when we are not even aware of it.

Now that's reassuring, knowing someone is watching over me when I can't look after myself. Knowing that when I catch myself worrying about my children, "getting left on the shelf," not enough money, diseases, etc., there's someone to whom I can commit everything, who will not fail or falter. There's someone who'll never call me a chatterbox because He loves to listen to me, and when He speaks to me, I feel a secure reassurance.

Unlike us, when He promises, He can *always* do it. When we have faith in Him, He does incredible things that could only have been possible in our wildest dreams.

He orders our steps and causes ALL things to work together for our good. Our joys, sorrows, disappointments, glories. Everything! Nothing goes to waste with God because He can turn everything around, even our mistakes, to serve a purpose, His purpose.

> *1 Chronicles 29: 11-13(MSG): "...to you, O God, belong the greatness and the might, the glory, the victory, the majesty, the splendor; Yes! Everything in heaven, everything on earth; the kingdom all yours! You've raised yourself high over all. Riches and glory come from you; you're ruler over all; You hold strength and power in the palm of your hand to build up and strengthen all...."*

His Love Letter to You

I love just like you because I made you in my image. I made you because I want you to choose me. I want to be first in all you do. My heart longs for you. My soul yearns for you.

All you want is in me. All you desire is in me. All there truly is can be found in me. Peace, joy, contentment, wealth, riches, honor, name it. I have it, and I'm ready to make it available to you, ready to lavish you with all, ready to overflow you with it in abundance.

I desire to satisfy you, but you have to come to me first. You must decide to be mine; it's not one to be forced. I want you to fall in love with me; I'm already in love with you.

But I don't want to be heartbroken, I don't want to be used, and that's why in our love relationship, I'll need to test you; know that your heart is genuine toward me. I want our love to be honest, weather the storm, grow, laugh, rejoice, cry, but ultimately be together, always.

I long for your embrace. I long for your breath in the place of prayer. I long to be by your side. I long for you to pursue me, be curious about me, look out for me, and care about me. I want to be filled with the joy of your love. Will you let me?

The Ceremony

I f your answer is yes, then please say this prayer with me out loud. "Lord Jesus, I'm so glad I finally met you. Thank you for finding me. I'm sorry for all the ways I wronged you before. Please, forgive me. I confess you as the Lord of my life now and always. I'm excited about our future together. I look forward to knowing you more, in Jesus name, Amen."

Welcome!

~⦾⦿⦾~

ow! It's great to have you as part of God's one big family! It would be great to know you decided for Him. Kindly email lovers@writeme.com. Remember that there is a party in heaven right now for you! The Bible is the best place to discover all about God's love. I recommend starting with the New Testament, particularly in this order, The Gospel of John, The Acts of the Apostles and the book of Romans. The New Testament will show you Jesus and how He lived, revealing His pattern for our lives. I find that "The Passion Translation" and "The Message" versions of the Bible are bursting with His passion for us and have an everyday language we can relate to. That's my recommendation. Feel free to explore. If you have a mobile device, "You Version" is a Bible app packed with wonders; I currently use it myself. Reading the bible in the morning and evening everyday is a good way to hear God speak to you.

You know when you first meet someone, and you're not sure which way the conversation is going to go? It can feel like that with prayer, at least initially. What's important to remember is that He's head over heels in love with you, and He knows you inside out, so please feel free and have a conversation with Him and pray. It may also feel one way at first because it's kind of awkward talking to someone you can't see, but it gets better with time because as you talk to Him and listen to Him, you'll hear Him talk back. He's gentle, funny, kind, reassuring, clear, and generally doesn't talk too much but what He says is enough. When you pray, you speak to God and this builds up communion/fellowship/relationship.

Also confess your faith, let people know you're now a believer in the Lord Jesus Christ, be proud of Him, he's already proud of you!

We were not designed to be isolated from other believers (lovers), and that's where the church comes in. So I encourage you to ask Him for the local church He'd want you to attend, people around you who you can study the scriptures and pray with, and some friends who also believe in Jesus with who you can walk and do life. Let them know you're new to the Christian faith, make new friends, and have fun serving Him. It is a new life, and committing to walking and finding out the new ways of enjoying a relationship with Jesus Christ is the next step.

When you give your life to Christ as you've done now, just like us after a wedding, we have a honeymoon period. You're in your honeymoon period with the lover of your soul, so enjoy it and make the most of it!

It's been an absolute delight to share God's love with you. I look forward to hearing your transformation and love stories with Him. Thank you!

Though You Are

Though you're the oldest being, you're the most attractive of all,

Though you're invisible, your presence is felt in all,

Though you're perfect, your acceptance of imperfection is unparalleled by all,

Though you're just, your display of mercy is incomprehensible by all,

Though you're the wisest, you're the humblest of all,

Though you could have everything, yet you don't have everything at all,

Though you're complete, yet you're incomplete without us all.

My Heart

My heart longs for each one of you to belong to me,

Regardless of who you are, where you've been and how you are,

There is a special place in me,

For each one of you.

Printed in Great Britain
by Amazon

81955725R00058